90-01355

J611
BER   9.95   old
        Berger, Gilda

The Human body.

Withdrawn

Other books you will enjoy:
Sharks by Gilda Berger
Dinosaurs by Daniel Cohen
Whales by Gilda Berger
Prehistoric Animals by Daniel Cohen
Stars and Planets by Christopher Lampton

The Human Body

By Gilda Berger
Illustrated by
Darcy May

Doubleday

New York   London   Toronto   Sydney   Auckland

Special thanks to Alan E. Nourse, M.D.,
for his careful review of the manuscript
and illustrations for this book.

Published by Doubleday, a division of
Bantam Doubleday Dell Publishing Group, Inc.
666 Fifth Avenue, New York, New York 10103

Doubleday and the portrayal of an anchor
with a dolphin are trademarks of Doubleday,
a division of Bantam Doubleday Dell
Publishing Group, Inc.

Library of Congress Cataloging-in-Publication Data
Berger, Gilda.
The human body.
Includes index.
Summary: An exploration of the parts and
functions of the human body which includes
the basic systems.
1. Body, Human—Juvenile literature.
[1. Body, Human.   2. Human physiology]
I. May, Darcy, ill.   II. Title.
QP37.B47 1989   611   87-27603
ISBN 0-385-24278-6
ISBN 0-385-24279-4 (lib. bdg.)

Book Design by November and Lawrence, Inc.

Text copyright © 1989 by Gilda Berger
Illustrations copyright © 1989 by Darcy May

A Visit to the Doctor

You and your parent arrive at the doctor's office. It is time for your yearly checkup. After a short wait, the nurse says, "Please come in. The doctor is ready now."

The doctor is pleased to see how much you've grown since last year. After chatting awhile, he leads you to the examining room and asks you to undress down to your underwear.

The doctor looks you over, head to toe, front and back. Next, he runs his fingers lightly over the bones of your neck and back. Are the bones lined up just right? He asks you to take a few steps. Is your posture good and are your feet straight? Are your muscles strong and healthy?

"Now," says the doctor, "hop up onto this table." From his pocket he takes out a light that looks like a pen. He holds your tongue down with a little flat stick and shines the light down your throat. Then, using other instruments, he peers into your eyes and ears.

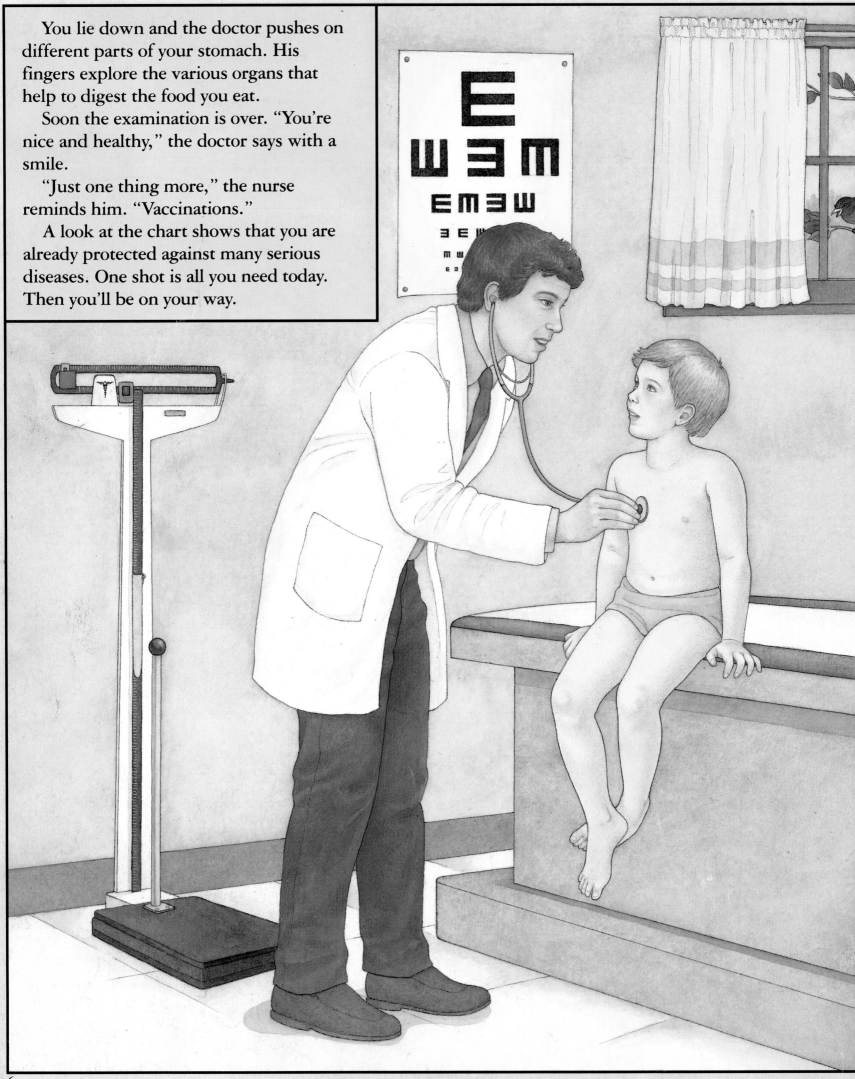

You lie down and the doctor pushes on different parts of your stomach. His fingers explore the various organs that help to digest the food you eat.

Soon the examination is over. "You're nice and healthy," the doctor says with a smile.

"Just one thing more," the nurse reminds him. "Vaccinations."

A look at the chart shows that you are already protected against many serious diseases. One shot is all you need today. Then you'll be on your way.

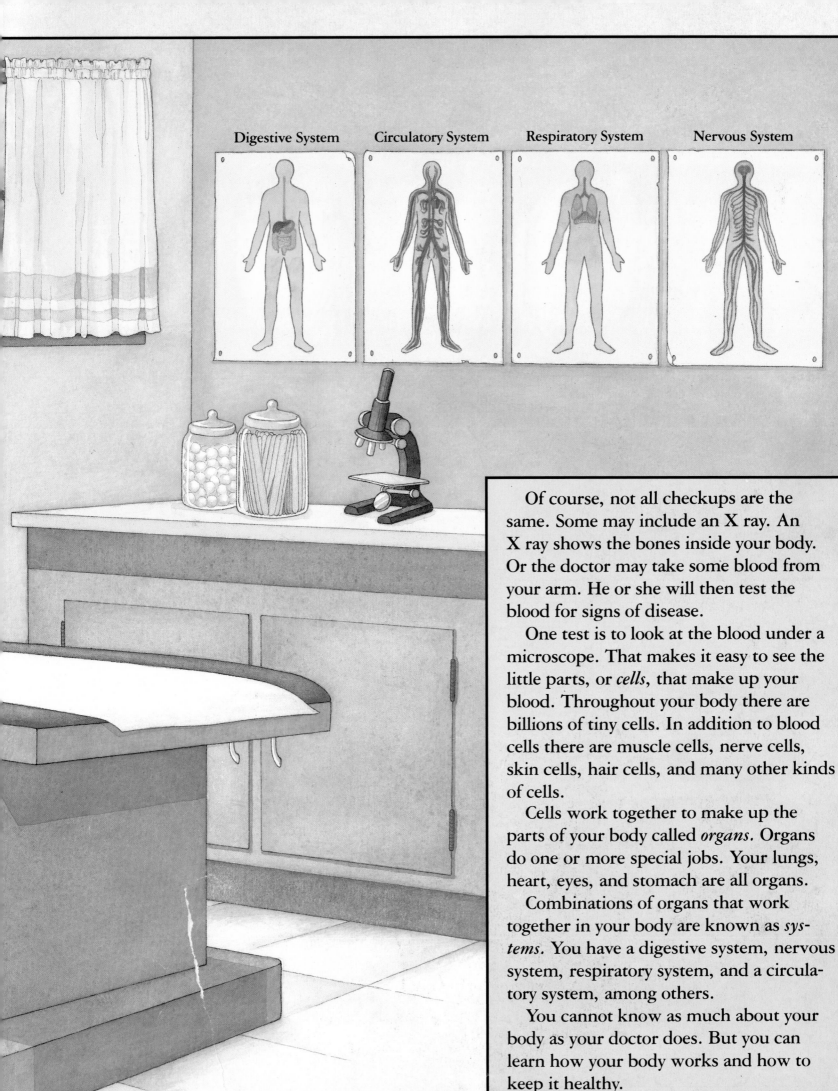

Digestive System   **Circulatory System**   **Respiratory System**   **Nervous System**

Of course, not all checkups are the same. Some may include an X ray. An X ray shows the bones inside your body. Or the doctor may take some blood from your arm. He or she will then test the blood for signs of disease.

One test is to look at the blood under a microscope. That makes it easy to see the little parts, or *cells,* that make up your blood. Throughout your body there are billions of tiny cells. In addition to blood cells there are muscle cells, nerve cells, skin cells, hair cells, and many other kinds of cells.

Cells work together to make up the parts of your body called *organs.* Organs do one or more special jobs. Your lungs, heart, eyes, and stomach are all organs.

Combinations of organs that work together in your body are known as *systems.* You have a digestive system, nervous system, respiratory system, and a circulatory system, among others.

You cannot know as much about your body as your doctor does. But you can learn how your body works and how to keep it healthy.

Bones and Muscles

Inside your body is a frame called a *skeleton*. The skeleton is made of bones. They give your body its shape. They hold you up. Without bones you would not be able to move. In fact, without them you would be more like a beanbag than a human being!

When you were born you had more than 300 bones. But since then some of the separate bones have grown together. By the time you graduate from high school, you will only have 206 bones in your body.

Some of your bones are for protection. The *skull* bone is like a hard hat to keep your brain from getting hurt. So are the twelve pairs of bones, called *ribs*, that curve around your chest. How many can you feel? The ribs are like a strong cage that guards your heart and lungs.

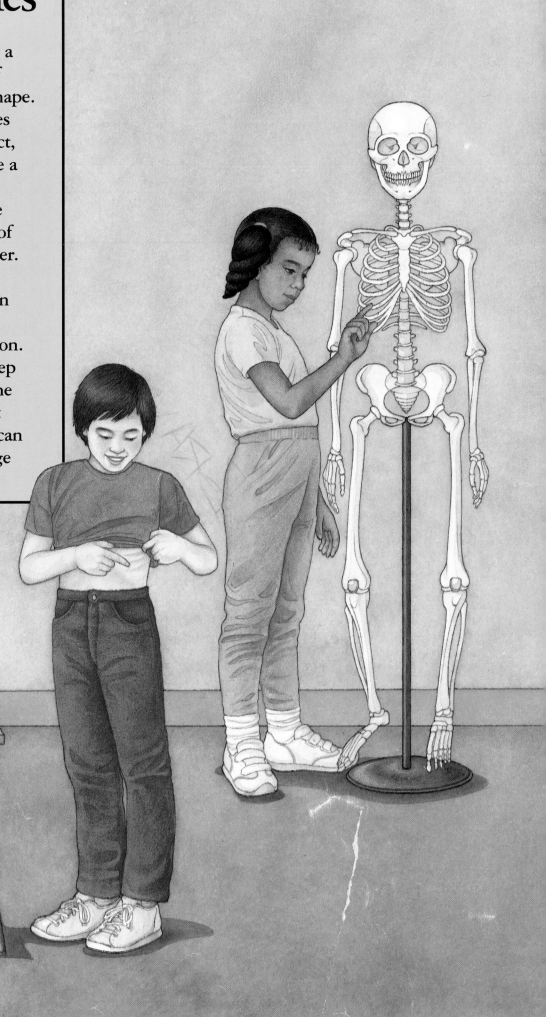

bone marrow

X ray

Other bones are for moving. Press hard on your upper and lower arms and you will feel the bones there. Do the same with the bones in your legs. You couldn't swing your arms or cross your legs without these bones.

The bone in your thigh, the *femur,* is the biggest bone in your body. The femur is like a sturdy pillar that helps hold up your body. In an adult this bone is about 20 inches long and 1 to 2 inches thick.

The smallest bone is inside your ear. The stirrup, or *stapes,* is just over one tenth of an inch long!

The outsides of most bones are very strong and hard and solid. The insides are full of holes like a sponge. This makes the bones very light. The spaces are filled with soft bone marrow. This is where the red blood cells and some white blood cells are made.

Even though they are strong, bones sometimes break. A slip on the ice or a fall off a bicycle can break, or *fracture,* a bone. The doctor takes an X ray of the broken bone and then pushes it back into place. A cast keeps the bone from moving while special cells start to heal the fracture. In time, the new growth hardens. The bone is as good as new.

Joints are places where one bone meets another. The elbow is a joint formed by bones of the upper and lower arm. The knee is the same kind of joint in the leg.

Without joints your body could not move or bend. There are more than 200 joints in your skeleton. Each hand alone has forty or so joints in the wrist and fingers. These joints let you tie your shoes, write with a pen, peel a banana—and do lots of other things.

Your backbone, or *spine,* is made up of thirty-three separate joints. These joints let you turn and bend in all directions, even making somersaults and cartwheels possible.

Ligaments hold the bones in place at the joints. When you bend a joint, the ligaments stretch and let the bones move. When you straighten the joint, they spring back like rubber bands.

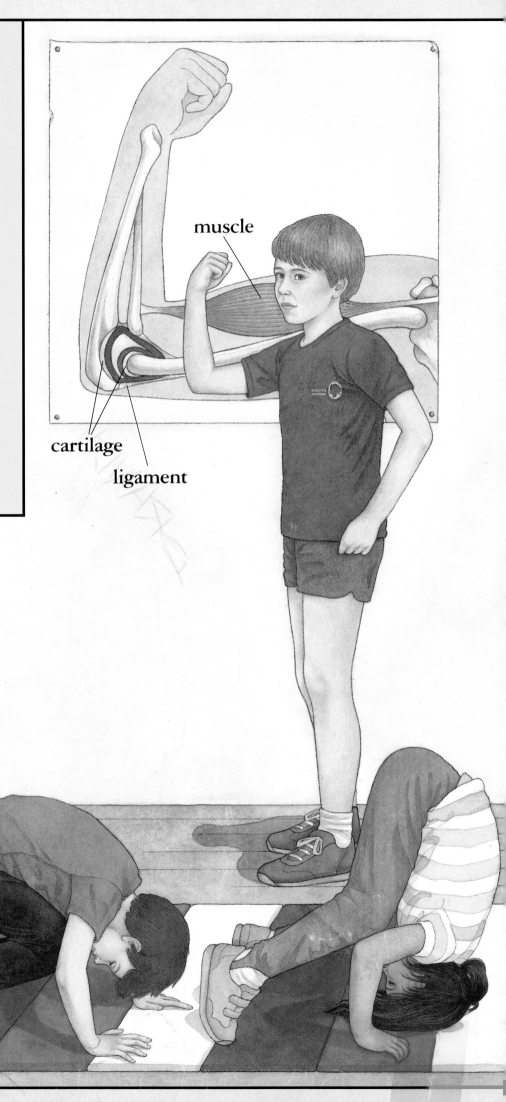

muscle

cartilage

ligament

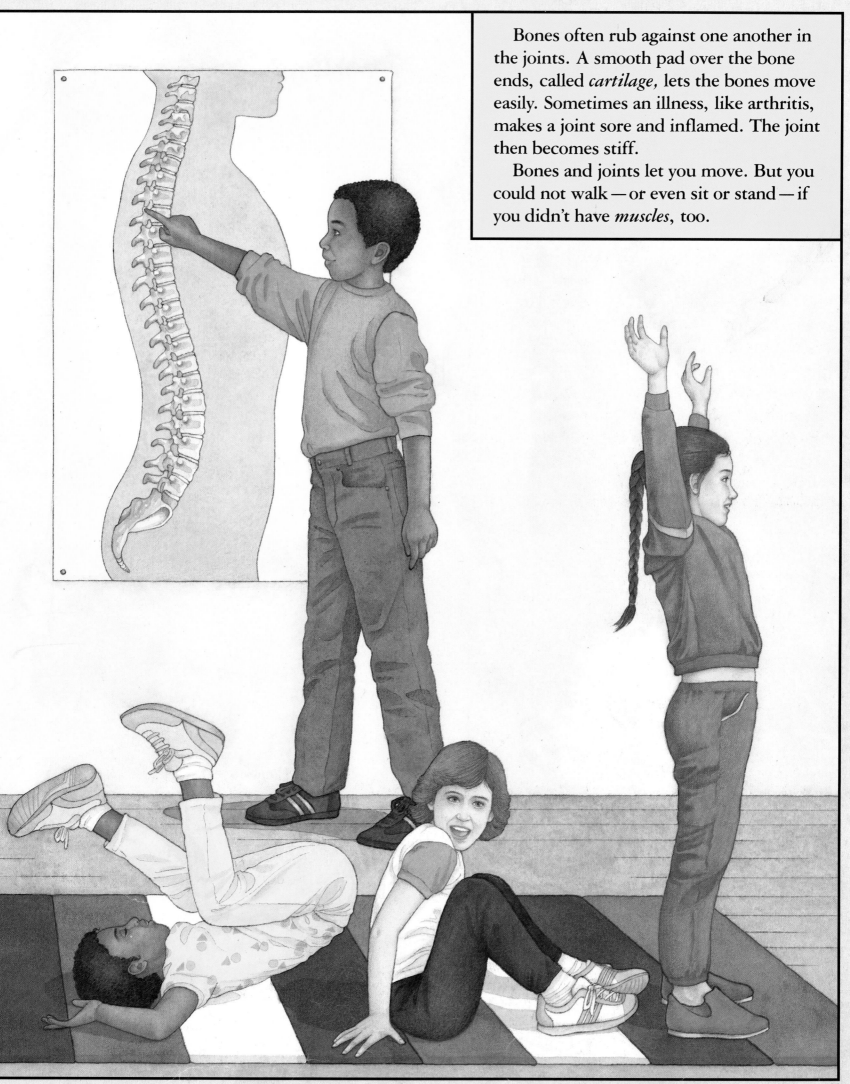

Bones often rub against one another in the joints. A smooth pad over the bone ends, called *cartilage,* lets the bones move easily. Sometimes an illness, like arthritis, makes a joint sore and inflamed. The joint then becomes stiff.

Bones and joints let you move. But you could not walk — or even sit or stand — if you didn't have *muscles,* too.

Over 600 muscles of every size and shape—flat, round, long, thin—are connected to your skeleton. Like cables, they pull on the bones to make them move. It takes hundreds of muscles just to take a single step!

Muscles work in pairs, pulling the bones back and forth. Each pair has a particular job to do. For every muscle that raises a bone, there is one to lower it.

A large pair of muscles in your upper arm are the *biceps* on top and *triceps* below. To lift your lower arm, the biceps tighten while the triceps loosen. To extend the arm, the biceps get loose while the triceps grow tight.

Some muscles are under your control. Since they are attached to the bones in your skeleton they are called *skeletal muscles*. You use these muscles every time you walk or run, clap your hands, or make a fist, smile, or frown.

Skeletal muscles get tired when you use them a lot. Then they need rest. But not for too long. Muscles must be used to stay strong. Regular exercise makes your muscles firmer and larger.

Sometimes you use a skeletal muscle so much that it becomes stiff and sore. You tell everyone you have a "charley horse." The name probably came from the use of "Charley" to refer to lame horses. Massage and gentle use of the muscle will get rid of most soreness.

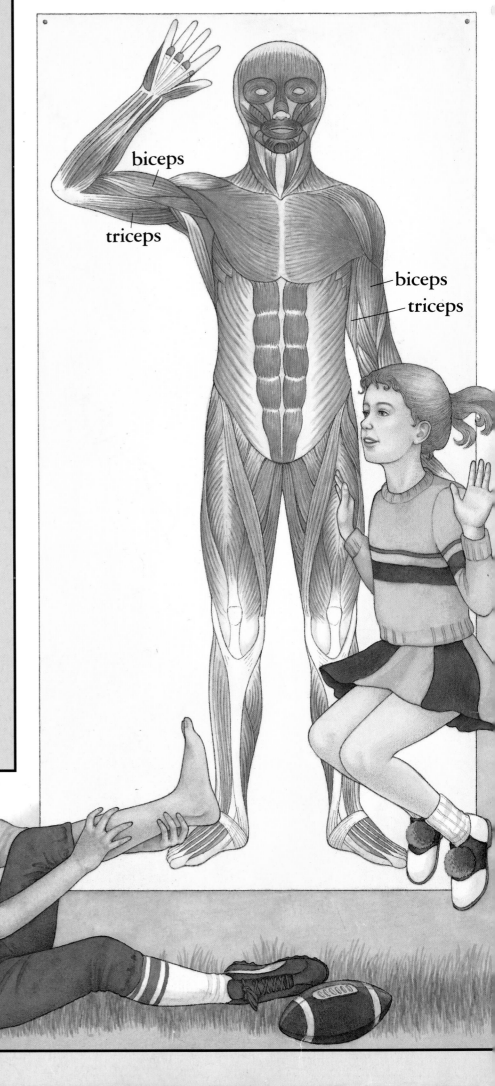

biceps

triceps

biceps

triceps

skeletal
muscle cells

smooth
muscle cells

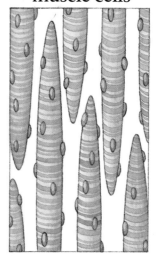
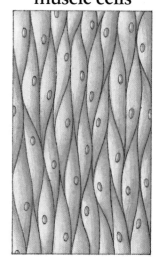

Other muscles are not under your control. These are the *smooth muscles.* Smooth muscles in the blood vessels, for example, can loosen to make them wide, or tighten to make them narrow. Smooth muscles in the throat help you swallow food. And in the stomach and intestines this kind of muscle helps digest your food.

The skeletal muscles are connected to the bones by lengths of tissue called *tendons.* Tendons are like ligaments, except that they are usually thicker and less elastic.

One strong tendon, the *Achilles tendon,* connects the muscle in the calf to the heel bone. You can touch the Achilles tendon at the back of your ankle. Flex and point your toe. Do you feel the tendon getting tighter and looser?

It is easy to see the tendons on the back of the hand. They run through the wrist and connect muscles of the arm to the fingers. Wiggle your fingers and you will see the tendons move.

Although things sometimes go wrong with the bones and muscles, the two systems work remarkably well. Every day you take nearly 20,000 steps—about eight miles! And your muscles do work equal to lifting dozens of tons! Few machines could do that much, day in and day out, without breaking down.

The Digestive System

"Eat this. It's good for you." That's what grown-ups always say. But do you know *why* food is good for you? And what happens to the food you eat?

Food is fuel for your body. Like other fuels — gasoline, wood, oil — food is burned to create energy. But unlike the other fuels, food does not burn in an engine or a fireplace. Instead, the burning of the food takes place — very, very slowly — inside your body's cells.

As the cells burn the food, they produce energy. We need energy for everything we do. It takes energy to run, to play — even to think. Growing taller, smarter, and bigger also takes a lot of energy.

But cells cannot "burn" foods the way they are. The hamburgers, pizza, and peanut-butter sandwiches you eat must first be broken down into tiny, tiny bits, or *molecules.* These molecules have to be small enough to enter your bloodstream. Then the blood is able to carry the separate molecules to cells around the body.

The way your body changes food into molecules is called *digestion.* The change-over takes place in a long tube in your body. Look at the picture of the digestive system. See how the tube starts at your *mouth.* Follow the food pipe, or *esophagus,* from your mouth to your *stomach.*

Notice how the tube then goes from the stomach to the part called the *small intestine.* When food reaches the small intestine, the *liver* and *pancreas* send special juices to the intestine. They break down

The Digestive System

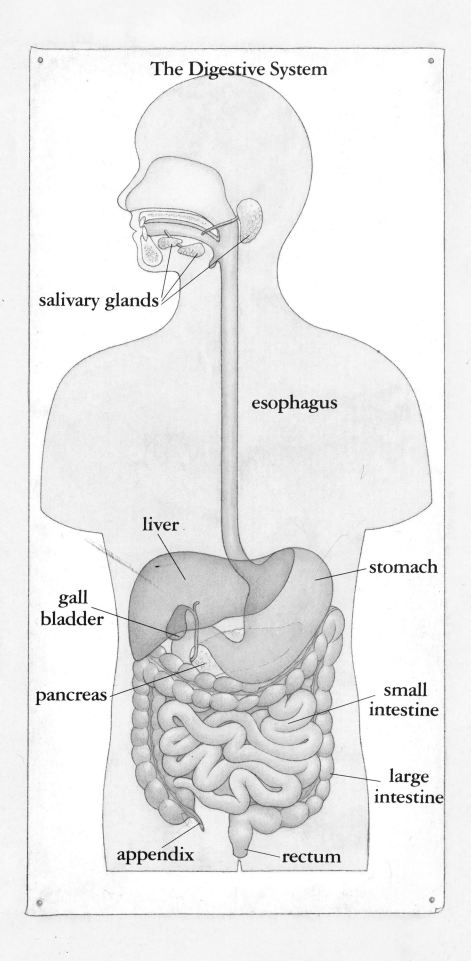

salivary glands

esophagus

liver

gall bladder

pancreas

stomach

small intestine

large intestine

appendix

rectum

the food even more. It takes four to six hours for the food to move through the small intestine. During its long journey, most of the food molecules pass through the intestine lining into your blood.

Can you spot where the small intestine becomes the *large intestine*? The large intestine is the last part of the digestive tube. Unused, waste food passes through your large intestine and out of your body through the end of this very long tube. Liquid wastes pass through your *kidneys* and *bladder*, and leave your body as urine.

Suppose you eat a slice of pizza. The digestion starts as soon as you put the food in your mouth. When you chew, you crush and grind the food into smaller pieces. At the same time a liquid, *saliva*, enters your mouth. The saliva contains special chemicals called *enzymes.* These enzymes start the job of breaking down the food bits into molecules.

Soon the crisp piece of pizza is soft and mushy. You swallow it and it passes into the esophagus. Here strong muscles force the food through the food pipe.

The food then enters your stomach. More enzymes, from the stomach walls, are added to the food here, while stomach muscles churn the food about. (If your stomach is empty, the movements of these muscles feel like hunger pains.)

After three or four hours, the mushy pizza passes into the small intestine. More enzymes flow in. The bits of food are broken down into tiny molecules. The pizza is finally in a form that your body can use.

The molecules are small enough to pass through the walls of the small intestine. They enter the blood vessels that line the small intestine. The blood carries the molecules to the cells. The cells take what they need to burn for energy and growth.

The Respiratory System

You breathe in and out every minute of your life — whether awake or asleep. Your life depends on it. You could live for weeks without food or a few days without water. But you could live only a few minutes without breathing.

Reading this book, you are breathing about twenty times a minute. Look closely at your chest. Do you see it rise up a little each time you take a breath? This makes your chest larger.

From your nose and mouth, air goes to your windpipe, or *trachea*. At its bottom end the pipe forms two branches, like an upside-down Y. The branches go into your two *lungs*. In the lungs, the pipes branch and branch again, just like the limbs of a

16

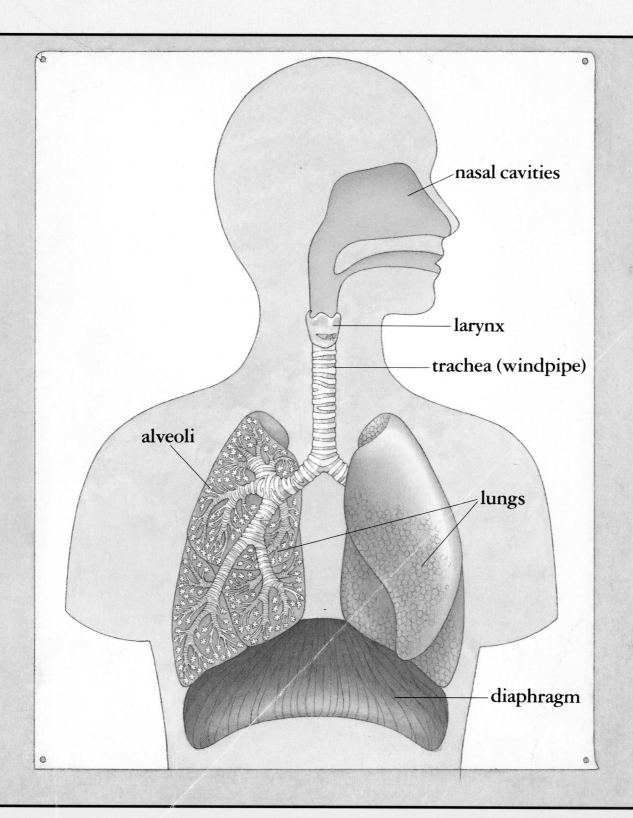

nasal cavities

larynx

trachea (windpipe)

alveoli

lungs

diaphragm

tree. Altogether, your nose and mouth, windpipe and lungs make up your *respiratory system*.

Each lung is made up of millions of tiny little sacs, or *alveoli*. The sacs are like tiny little balloons. All of the sacs together hold about as much air as a basketball.

Very small blood vessels surround each sac. The oxygen in the air passes right through the thin walls of the sacs and into the blood vessels. The blood then carries the oxygen to cells all over your body.

The cells use the oxygen to burn the food molecules. This produces a waste gas, carbon dioxide (CO_2). The blood picks up the CO_2 and brings it back to the lungs. The CO_2 passes into the tiny sacs. And finally, you breathe out the CO_2.

As you probably know, you don't always breathe at the same speed. You breathe faster after running, climbing stairs, or playing hard at an active sport. You may take as many as sixty breaths a minute when you are exercising.

Why do you breathe so hard while you are running, for example? Your muscles and other parts of your body need more oxygen. Breathing faster gets that extra oxygen into your cells. When you stop the activity, you need less oxygen. So you breathe more slowly.

If you get lots of exercise, your lungs become able to take in more air with every breath. Then you can run or play longer and harder without panting for breath.

Each time you take a breath, three things happen to the air that enters your nose.

The air is cleaned. Tiny hairs in your nose work to trap the little bits of dirt and germs you breathe in with the air.

The air is made slightly wet. Damp passages within your nose add moisture to the air.

And the air is warmed. Blood flowing through the lining of the nose gives off heat.

Despite these safeguards, germs sometimes get into your respiratory system. The germs start to grow in your nose, throat, and lungs. You say you have a cold.

To fight the cold, the linings of your nose and throat swell. They form a thick, clear liquid, *mucus*, to wash away the germs. The mucus builds up and blocks the air passages. The result can be a stuffy nose and a bad cough.

Some substances in the air can damage the lungs. Cigarette smoke is one example. The gases, tars, and nicotine in the smoke irritate the lungs. The air passages get narrower and narrower. The lungs have to work very hard to take in oxygen and exhale carbon dioxide.

After years of smoking, a person can develop lung cancer. Sometimes the cancer can be removed by surgery. The person may then live with only one lung.

To keep your lungs healthy—
 breathe fresh air,
 exercise hard,
 and stay away from cigarettes.

The Heart and Blood System

Did you know there is a tube inside your body that is 60,000 miles long? This "tube" carries the blood around your body and keeps you alive. It is your *blood system*.

At the center of this system is your *heart.* Your heart is a powerful muscle. It has to be. The heart pumps, or beats, all the time. It beats day and night, when you are asleep or awake.

The heart pumps the blood to the lungs, back to the heart, out to every part of the body and back to the heart again. Each round trip takes about twenty seconds. During your life your heart will beat about three billion times!

Red cells in the blood bring digested food molecules and oxygen to all parts of your body. These blood cells also pick up waste carbon dioxide from the body cells and carry it back to the lungs. When you breathe out, you exhale the carbon dioxide.

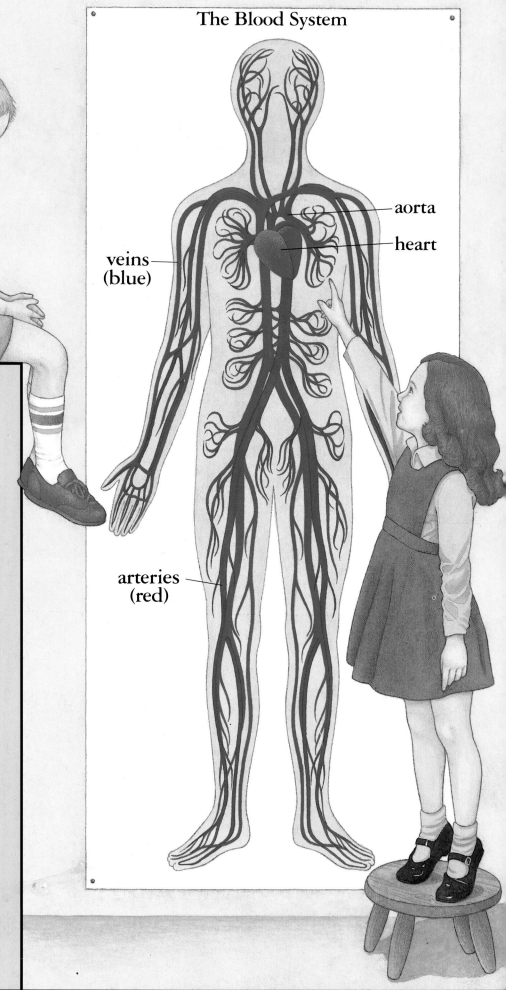

The Blood System

aorta

heart

veins
(blue)

arteries
(red)

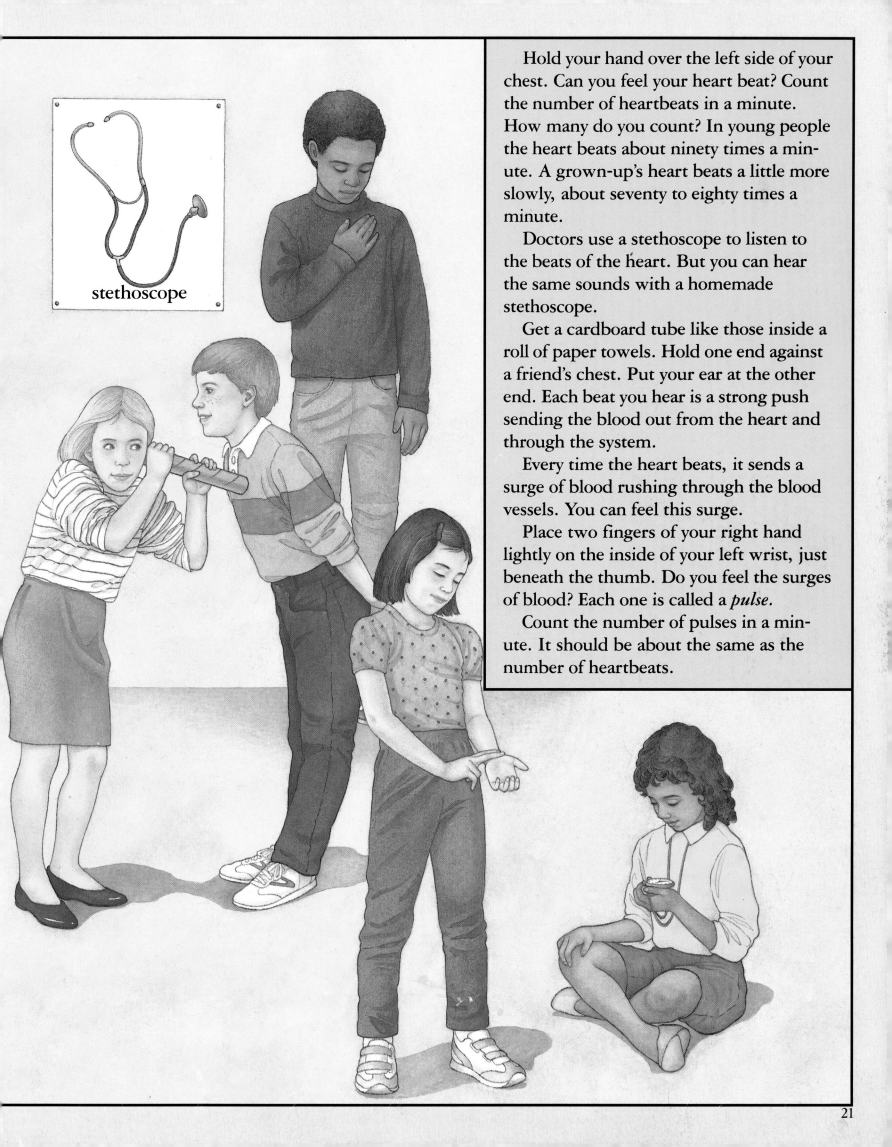

stethoscope

Hold your hand over the left side of your chest. Can you feel your heart beat? Count the number of heartbeats in a minute. How many do you count? In young people the heart beats about ninety times a minute. A grown-up's heart beats a little more slowly, about seventy to eighty times a minute.

Doctors use a stethoscope to listen to the beats of the heart. But you can hear the same sounds with a homemade stethoscope.

Get a cardboard tube like those inside a roll of paper towels. Hold one end against a friend's chest. Put your ear at the other end. Each beat you hear is a strong push sending the blood out from the heart and through the system.

Every time the heart beats, it sends a surge of blood rushing through the blood vessels. You can feel this surge.

Place two fingers of your right hand lightly on the inside of your left wrist, just beneath the thumb. Do you feel the surges of blood? Each one is called a *pulse*.

Count the number of pulses in a minute. It should be about the same as the number of heartbeats.

But pulses and heartbeats do not always stay the same. Your heart beats faster when you exercise. It also speeds up when you are angry, scared, or excited. These extra beats bring more oxygen-rich blood to the muscles. When you stop exercising and grow calm, your heart slows down. Also during sleep the heart pumps less blood per minute.

The blood vessels that carry the blood away from the heart and to the rest of the body are called *arteries.* They divide into smaller and smaller blood vessels. The smallest ones are the *capillaries.* From the capillaries, the blood flows into the *veins.* The veins bring the blood back to the heart.

Most hearts keep beating all life long without trouble. But once in a while something goes wrong.

Sometimes an artery in the heart itself gets clogged. It is hard for the blood to get through. The person has a *heart attack.* Often heart attacks can be prevented by eating a low fat diet—lots of fruits, vegetables, whole-grain breads, lean meats, fish and poultry. Getting plenty of exercise also helps keep you fit.

Sometimes the timing of the heartbeats is not right. Doctors must set the speed, or pace, for the beats of the heart. A surgeon may put a small artificial *pacemaker* inside the patient's chest. The pacemaker sends tiny electric shocks to the heart. The shocks keep the heart beating.

But your blood is more than a delivery and pickup system for the cells. Your blood also fights off disease germs. Certain cells in the blood—the *white blood cells*—attack germs that invade your body. They surround the germs and swallow them up.

There are also chemicals in your blood called *antibodies.* The antibodies help the white blood cells kill disease germs. The white cells and the antibodies make up your body's *immune system.*

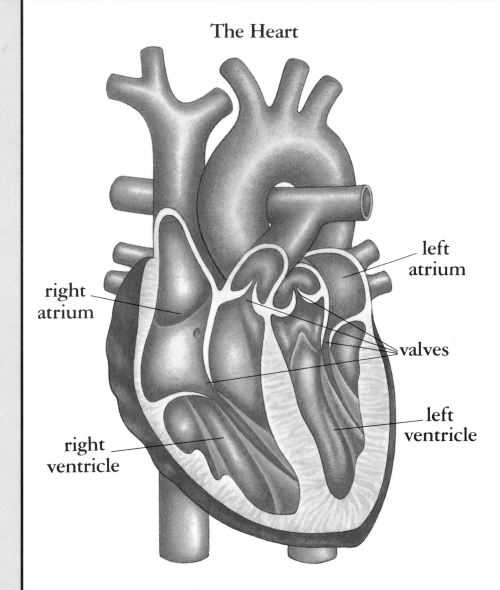

The Heart

right atrium

left atrium

valves

right ventricle

left ventricle

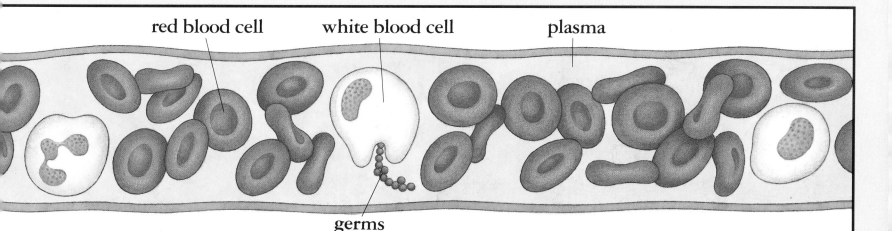

red blood cell   white blood cell   plasma

germs

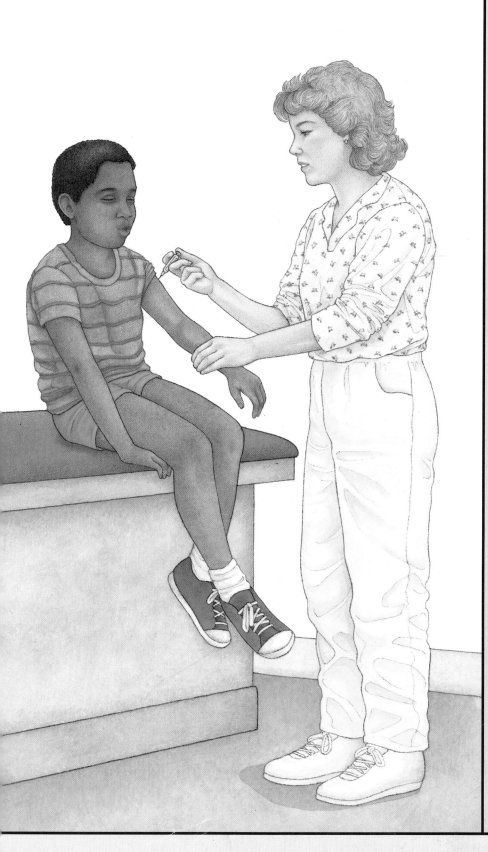

The immune system wages long-term war against certain germs. Suppose you get measles. White cells attack the germs. Antibodies join in the fight. Soon you are feeling better. But the antibodies stay in your blood, sometimes forever. If measles germs ever enter your body again, the antibodies will fight them off. You have long-term *immunity* to measles.

Doctors have a way of giving you long-term immunity to certain diseases you haven't had. The method is called *vaccination*. A vaccination "tricks" your body into making protective antibodies against certain diseases. Your body produces the antibodies without having the disease.

Vaccines are not all alike. Some have disease germs in them that are dead. The vaccine against whooping cough is an example. Other vaccines contain disease germs that are alive, but very weak. The polio vaccine is this kind. When either kind of these weak germs enter your body they won't make you sick. Instead they cause your body to make antibodies to fight whooping cough or polio.

Which vaccinations have you had? Polio? Mumps? Measles? Diphtheria? Tetanus? Rubella? Whooping cough? You should be immunized against all these diseases.

The antibodies produced by some vaccinations do not last very long. So it may be necessary to have *booster* doses or shots from time to time. Boosters help your body's immune system keep you healthy.

The Brain and Nervous System

Can you...

...touch the tip of your nose with your finger?

...remember what you ate for lunch yesterday?

...wiggle the toes of your left foot?

...add 12, 6, and 17 in your head?

...think of a favorite song and recall the way it makes you feel?

Each of these actions is different. Yet they all depend on your *central nervous system* (CNS). The CNS includes the *brain*, the *spinal cord*, and the *nerves*.

Your CNS is a little like a very busy telephone network. The brain is the switchboard. It is in charge of receiving and sending thousands of messages day and night from all over the body.

The spinal cord is the main cable. It extends from the base of the brain down the length of the back. The spinal cord contains thousands of separate nerves.

The nerves are like the telephone wires. They carry messages from every part of the body to and from your brain. Messages to the brain travel through the *sensory*

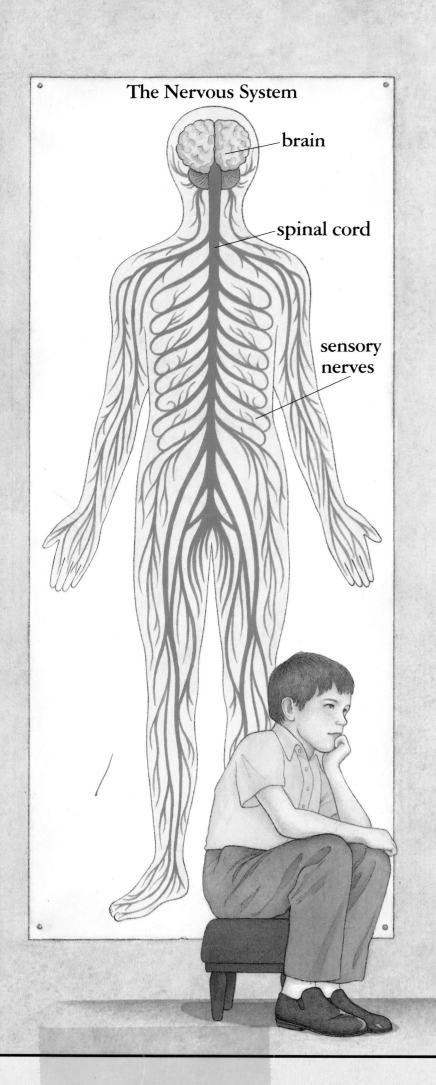

The Nervous System

brain

spinal cord

sensory
nerves

nerves. Messages from the brain go out through the *motor* nerves.

Let's say you decide to watch TV. Sensory nerves from your eyes to your brain tell you where the TV is. Signals flash from your brain and through the spinal cord to many different motor nerves. They direct your muscles to walk to the set, turn it on, get the right channel, and sit down. And finally your brain orders your eyes and ears to shut out everything else but the sound and picture of the TV.

Your CNS does all these complicated things in a very direct way. It just sends small electrical signals from one nerve to another. One of these signals can flash the entire length of your body in a tiny fraction of a second. This lets the CNS handle the most complicated messages and do the most difficult tasks in the shortest possible time.

The *endocrine glands* help the nervous system control the body's activities. These glands give off chemicals known as *hormones*. Hormones affect the way parts of your body function and grow.

Your brain begins growing at birth. It grows a little bit each year until you are about twenty. At full size your brain will weigh about three pounds. Also, the more you use your brain, the better it will work.

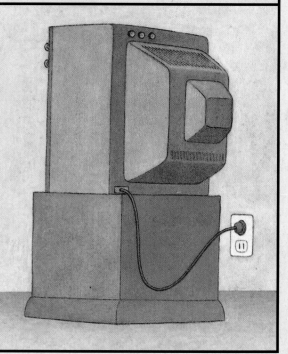

The brain has three main parts. The biggest and uppermost section is the *cerebrum*. You use your cerebrum to think, to talk, to understand, and to remember things. The cerebrum also takes care of all the things you do that are under your control. Everything from lifting a finger to taking a step, from playing guitar to swimming, is done by signals from the cerebrum. The signals travel through motor nerves to the correct body muscles.

The left side of the cerebrum mostly controls reading, writing, speaking, math and science skills. The right is the artistic side. It helps you picture things in your mind and use your imagination. Which side of *your* brain is stronger?

Below the cerebrum is the much smaller *cerebellum*. The cerebellum makes sure your muscles work just right; not too much or too little. It makes sure you can walk a straight line, climb a ladder, or do anything else that takes coordination and balance.

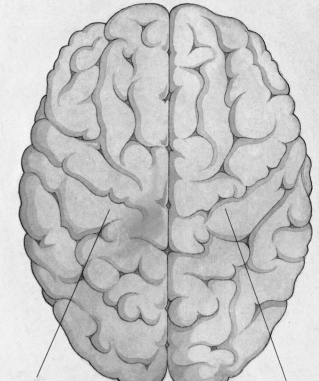

The left brain is your intellectual side

The right brain is your creative side

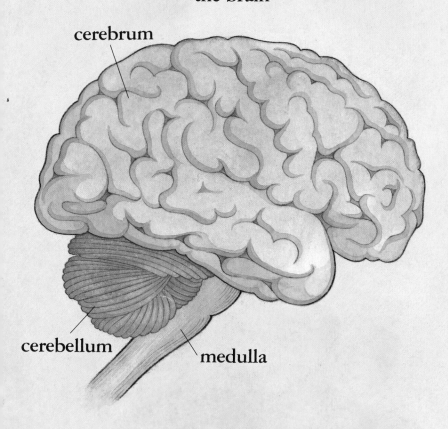

the brain

cerebrum

cerebellum

medulla

The brain stem, or *medulla*, is the busiest part of the brain. All back-and-forth messages go through the brain stem. And most actions that you don't think about start here. Your heartbeat, breathing, digestion, and other automatic activities are guided by the medulla.

During sleep your brain is less active. But it never stops working completely. You dream, for example, even though you're asleep. Some people even walk and talk in their sleep!

Sleep gives the cells in the nervous system a chance to renew their energy. Sleep helps refresh you. It keeps you from feeling tired the next day.

Few things in nature are more remarkable than the body's nervous system. From the moment you are born until you die it controls your every thought, feeling, and action. Without it you could not move a muscle, solve a puzzle, write a letter, or get the point of a joke. Life would be much less fun!

The Senses

Lots of things are happening to you right now. You are reading this book. You are hearing sounds from inside the room and outside. You are feeling the weight of the book and the smoothness of the paper. You are picking up the smells in the air. You may even be tasting the flavor of a snack or a piece of gum.

All this information comes to you through your five basic sense organs: eyes, ears, nose, tongue, and skin. Each one gets a particular kind of message from the outside world. Each sends the message along nerves to your brain, which decides what it means.

Your *eye* is the organ for seeing. It works this way. Suppose you watch a sunset. Light given off by the sun passes first through the *cornea*, a clear covering that protects your eye. The light then goes through the *pupil*, the small dark "window" in the center of your eye. All around the pupil is the colored part of your eye, called the *iris*.

Small muscles open the pupil when the light is dim. More light entering your eyes helps you to see better. The same muscles make the pupil smaller when there is too

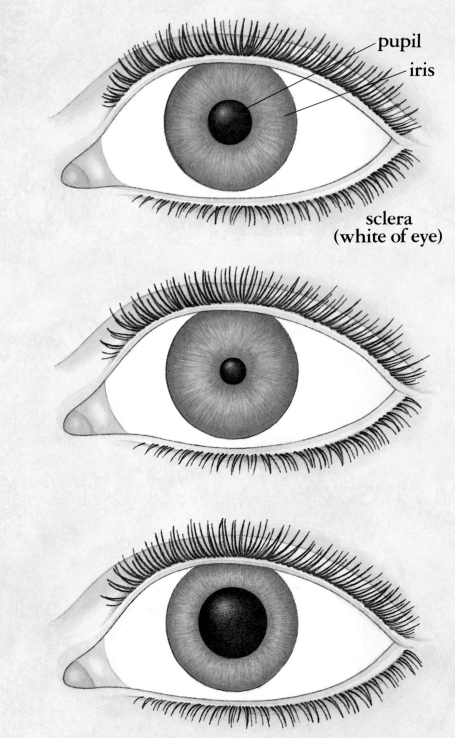

pupil
iris
sclera
(white of eye)

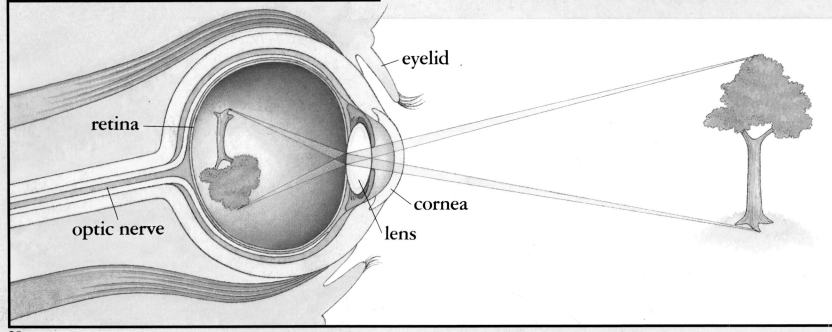

eyelid
retina
optic nerve
cornea
lens

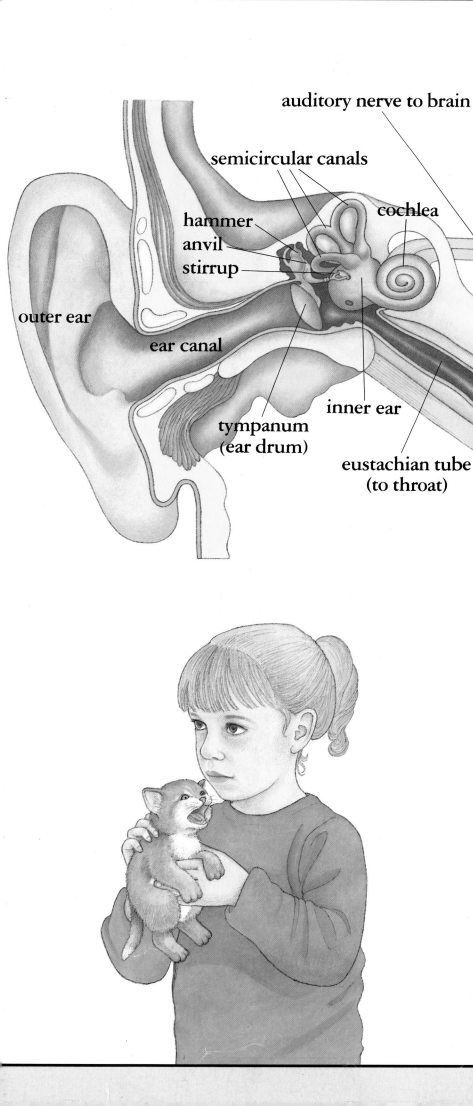

auditory nerve to brain

semicircular canals

cochlea

hammer
anvil
stirrup

outer ear

ear canal

inner ear

tympanum
(ear drum)

eustachian tube
(to throat)

much light. Very bright light can be blinding.

Behind the pupil and iris is the *lens*. The lens brings the image of the sunset to a focus on the back wall of your eyeball, or *retina*. But the lens makes the picture of the sunset fall upside down on the retina. How is this picture turned right side up? The retina has millions of nerve endings. Each ending picks up a tiny speck of the image. The nerves then send a signal through the *optic nerve* to the brain. Your brain changes the signals into a right-side-up image that you know as a sunset.

Your *ear* is the organ of hearing. The saucer-like shape of the *outer ear* gathers the sound waves in the air—from a purring kitten to a jet plane.

A short tunnel, called the *ear canal*, brings the sound waves to the delicate *eardrum*. The eardrum looks like a tiny drumhead. The sound waves make the eardrum jiggle, or vibrate. The vibrations pass to the three smallest bones in the body —the *hammer*, *anvil*, and *stirrup*. They are found in your *middle ear*.

The three bones pass the vibrations along to the *inner ear*. Inside is the liquid-filled *cochlea*, which is shaped like a snail shell. Nerve endings in the cochlea sense the vibrations and send signals to your brain. The brain gets the signals and you hear and understand the sounds.

You have another kind of sense in the ear. It is the sense of balance. Inside the inner ear are some curved loops that are filled with liquid. The loops are called *semicircular canals*. They keep you from leaning or falling down when you walk, stand, or sit.

Twirling around creates waves in the semicircular canals. The liquid "tickles" the nerve endings. You feel dizzy. When you stop spinning the liquid levels out. The tickling stops and you feel steady again.

The sense of touch or feel works through your *skin*. Nerve endings for touch are found all over your body. Each ending reacts to only one sensation — heat, cold, pain, touch, or pressure. Whatever you touch, the great number of nerves in the body let you know what it is.

Some parts of your body have more nerve endings than others. Your hands are a good example. In places the hands have over thirteen hundred nerve endings per square inch. That is one reason you use your hands to touch things, and not your elbows, knees, or nose!

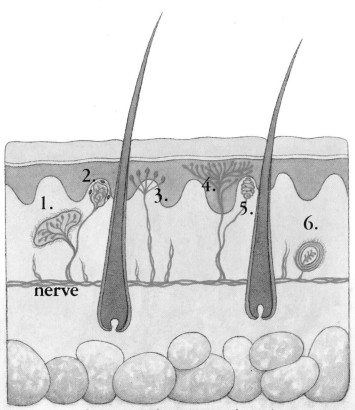

nerve endings: 1. heat   4. pain
                2. cold   5. light touch
                3. touch 6. pressure

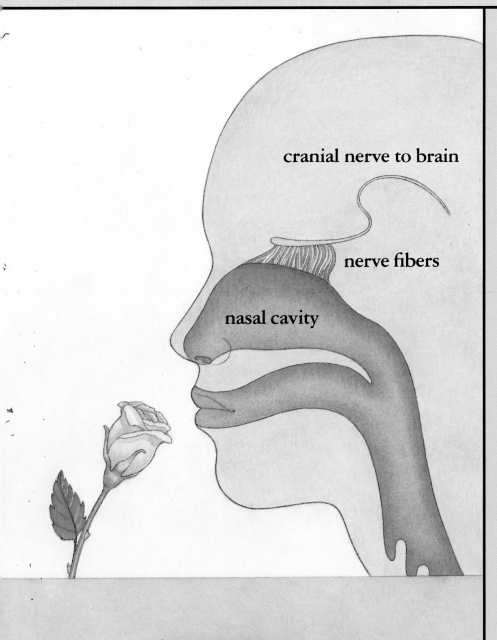

cranial nerve to brain

nerve fibers

nasal cavity

Your *nose*, of course, is for smelling. Odors come into your nose with the air. In the back of your nose are thousands of tiny hairs. They are connected to a nerve that runs to your brain. When the smell enters your nose, the nerve sends the message to your brain. And your brain tells you what the smell is.

Your *tongue* is the organ of taste. The bumps on your tongue are *taste buds*. They are the endings of the tasting nerves. Near the tip of your tongue are the taste buds for sweet and salty. Those for sour at the sides. And the ones for bitter are at the back.

The different taste buds are located on your tongue like towns on a map. Draw a tongue shape on a piece of paper. Then "map" the taste buds for sweet, salty, sour, and bitter this way: Place a pinch of sugar in three places on your tongue—on the tip, the side, and the back. Write "sugar" on the spot where the sweet taste is strongest. Do the same with the following foods: A pinch of salt. A piece of sour pickle. A square of bitter chocolate. Does your picture of the taste buds on your tongue look like this one?

Do you ever think how wonderful your senses are? And can you guess how your senses help you enjoy the world you live in?

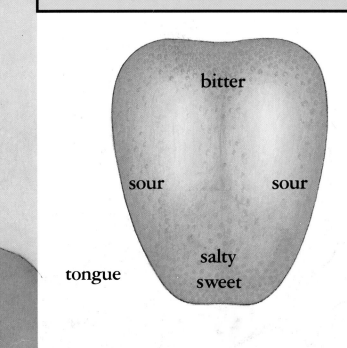

bitter

sour   sour

salty
tongue   sweet

The Skin

What part of your body...

...wraps you in a waterproof cover?

...stretches and folds?

...grows larger as you grow larger?

The answer, of course, is your *skin*!

The skin has two layers. The outside layer, or *epidermis*, is thin and strong and without blood vessels. Sometimes you scrape yourself. It stings and smarts but doesn't bleed. Then you know you've only hurt your epidermis.

Mostly the epidermis is made up of dead skin cells. Drying yourself with a towel actually rubs off little bits of epidermis.

The inside layer of the skin is the *dermis.* The dermis is far thicker than the epidermis. And the dermis is full of blood vessels. A cut that bleeds tells you that you have broken into the inside layer of the skin.

You should wash every cut with soap and water. This gets rid of the dirt and germs. Then put on a bandage to keep it clean.

In time the cut will stop bleeding. You'll see a clear, sticky liquid oozing out. It covers the cut and dries, making a crust called a *scab*.

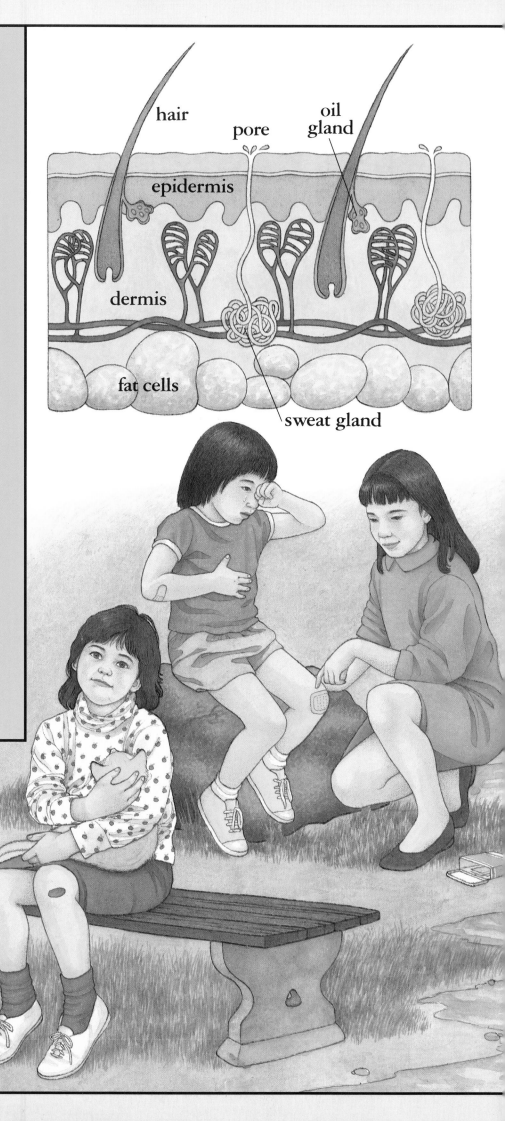

hair

pore

oil gland

epidermis

dermis

fat cells

sweat gland

The scab keeps germs out until new skin can grow. Then the scab falls off. Pulling a scab off is never a good idea. Germs can get into the cut and it will take longer to heal, possibly leaving a scar.

There are other ways in which your skin protects you. On summer days or when you're exercising, you get hot and sweaty. Sweat is a mixture of water and salt that comes out of your skin. As the sweat dries, it cools you off.

Sweat forms in tiny *sweat glands* in your skin. It gets out through very small holes in the skin called *pores.* Sweat glands and pores are found all over your body.

You can lose as much as ten quarts of water on a steamy day. This can make you feel faint or dizzy. For that reason, it's good to drink lots of water in the summer or after hard exercise.

Do you know that hair is part of your skin? And that your whole body is covered with little hairs, even though you can't see them? Only two places have no hair. They are the palms of your hands and the soles of your feet.

Each hair grows out of a little hole called a *follicle*. The follicle has oil in it to make the hair soft and shiny. The oil helps keep the skin from drying out and cracking. It also stops water from getting through.

About 100,000 hairs grow on your head. The hairs form a thick mat that can soften some blows. Each hair grows a quarter of an inch or more every month.

Fingernails and toenails are part of your skin, too. Strong and stiff, they protect your fingers and toes. Nails are like hair. They keep growing all the time. But hair and nails are made of dead skin cells. That is why it doesn't hurt when they are cut.

The skin on your fingertips is very special. It is covered with loops and lines of raised ridges. The ridges are like the tread on car tires. Just as tire treads help cars hold the road, the ridges help fingers grasp objects.

If you put ink on a fingertip and press it on paper, you get a fingerprint. No two people, even identical twins, have the exact same fingerprints. Police use fingerprints to find individuals they are looking for.

In a way, your skin is like a radiator that keeps you warm. On a cold day the blood

vessels in your skin become very narrow. Less blood flows through the skin. That means less heat is lost to the air. You feel warmer.

Your skin is also like a refrigerator that keeps you cool. When you get hot, the blood vessels in the skin become wider. More blood circulates through your skin. Heat from the warm blood escapes into the air. This cools your whole body.

In bright sunshine your skin makes extra bits of brown color, called *melanin*. Melanin makes you look suntanned. The tan is a screen that blocks out some of the sun's rays.

Everyone's skin makes melanin. People from hot lands usually have a lot of melanin; they are dark-skinned. Those from lands with little sunshine have fewer bits of melanin; they are fair. Brown-eyed people have more melanin than those with blue eyes.

Sometimes the melanin forms spots on the skin known as *freckles*. Except for the different amounts of melanin, the skin of every person is the same.

Too much time in the bright sun can cause cancers to grow in the skin. Sun-blocking lotion helps prevent cancers. The lotion screens out those rays that can cause the disease.

A doctor can tell a lot just by looking at your skin. Smooth, elastic skin is a sign of good health. It means you are eating a balanced diet. A rash may signal an infection in the body, and a flush sometimes indicates a fever.

Your skin, it seems, does more than just cover you.

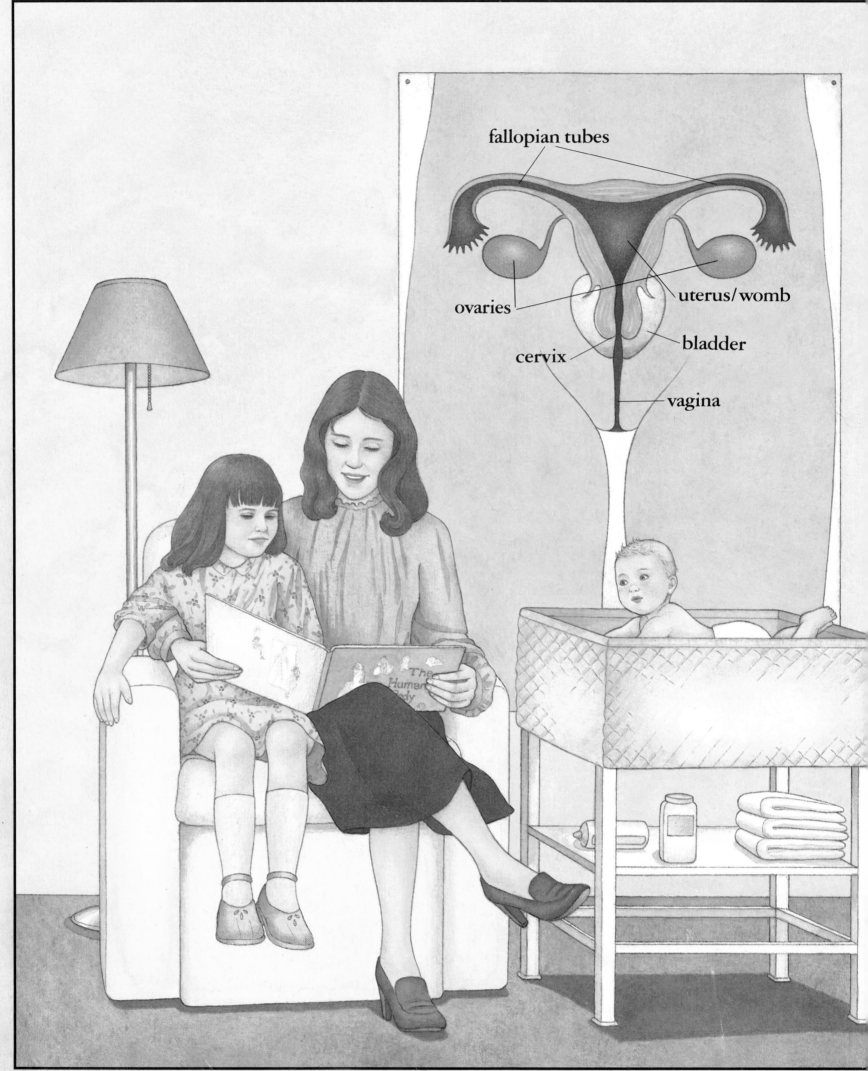

fallopian tubes

ovaries

uterus/womb

cervix

bladder

vagina

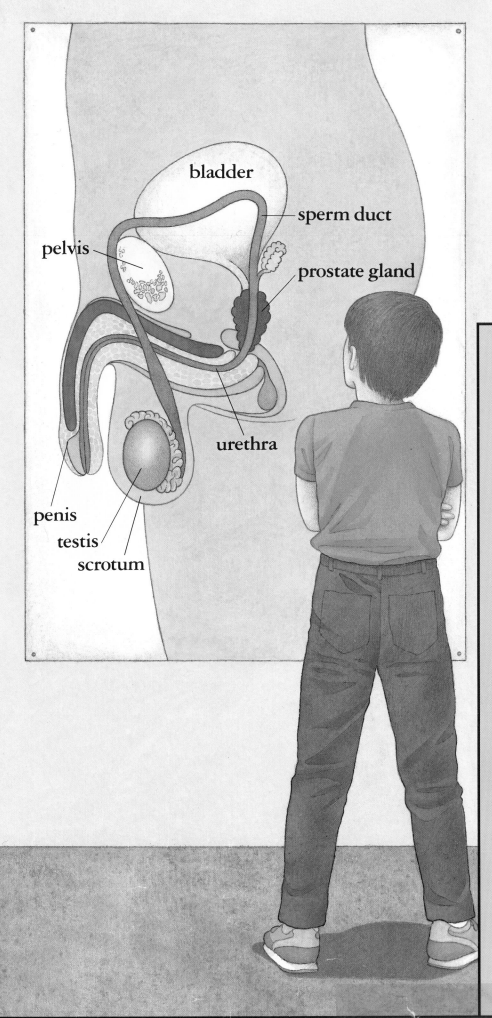

bladder

sperm duct

pelvis

prostate gland

urethra

penis

testis

scrotum

The Reproductive System

Boys and girls are basically alike. Their organs and systems work in just about the same ways. But one system is very different. It is the *reproductive system*, which grown-ups use to have babies.

Leading inside a girl's body is a little passageway called the *vagina*. At the end of the vagina is a hollow ball about the size of your fist. It is the *womb* or *uterus*. The uterus holds the baby while it is growing inside the mother.

Two tubes called the *fallopian tubes* lead from the uterus to the *ovaries*. Each of the two ovaries is oval in shape and about an inch long. Every girl is born with more than 200,000 sex cells in her ovaries. They are called eggs, or *ova*.

A boy has a tube-like organ on the out-side of his body. It is called the *penis*. In back of the penis is a small pouch known as the *scrotum*. The scrotum contains two *testes*. Between the ages of ten and four-teen, the testes begin to produce millions of male sex cells, called *sperm*.

As girls and boys enter their teens, their bodies change in lots of ways. This change is called *puberty.* At puberty, girls begin to develop breasts, hair in different places on their body, and wider hips. Boys grow larger in size, develop a deeper voice, and get more hair on their face and body.

Some of the changes get the body ready to produce a baby. One change in young women is that the ovaries start to release their eggs leading to a monthly flow of blood from the body called *menstruation.* And one change in young men is that the testes begin to produce sperm.

All babies get started the same way. One sperm cell and one egg cell come together inside the woman's body. How does this happen?

A man and a woman lie very close together. The man's penis gets stiff and fits inside the woman's vagina. Sperm cells move from the testes through the penis and into the vagina. The cells move up the vagina into the uterus. From there they go into the fallopian tubes, which lead to the ovaries.

Once a month, an egg moves down a tube from the ovary. If a sperm meets the egg in the tube, they may join together. The sperm has *chromosomes* that carry features of the father. The egg has chromosomes that carry features of the mother.

The two cells become a single cell. From this cell will grow a totally new human being.

Very soon the cell divides and becomes two new cells. Each one is exactly like the other. The two cells divide and become four new cells. The cells keep dividing until there is a small clump of very tiny cells.

The bunch of cells moves down the tube into the uterus. It attaches itself to the inside of the uterus. Here the cells keep on growing and dividing.

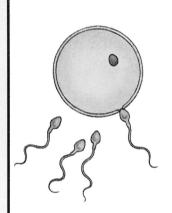
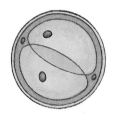
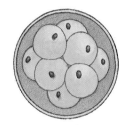
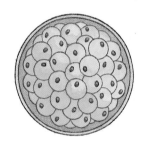
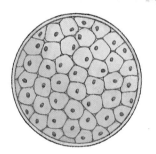

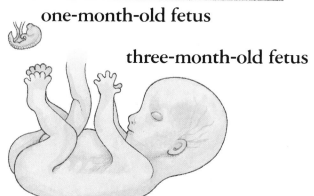

one-month-old fetus

three-month-old fetus

Soon millions of cells are growing in one place to make a baby. At this stage it is called a *fetus*. A one-month-old fetus is only a quarter of an inch long. Yet it is beginning to form a body. The fetus receives food and gets rid of waste through an organ in the mother's uterus called the *placenta*. The flexible tube that connects the fetus to the placenta is the *umbilical cord*. Your belly button marks the place where the umbilical cord was attached to your body before you were born.

After three months, the fetus measures three inches—about as long as a stick of gum. It has almost every part of its body in place. Over the next six months it will just keep growing bigger and stronger.

At nine months or so the fetus is ready to be born. The uterus pushes the fetus down into the vagina. The vagina stretches and the baby comes out.

Every once in a while a baby cannot come into the world this way. So the doctor removes it from the uterus in an operation called a *Caesarian* section.

All of us are born one of these two ways. We are all built along the same lines. And all of us have bones and muscles, organs and systems that work in the same general way. Yet everyone is special and different. There is no one in the world exactly like you!

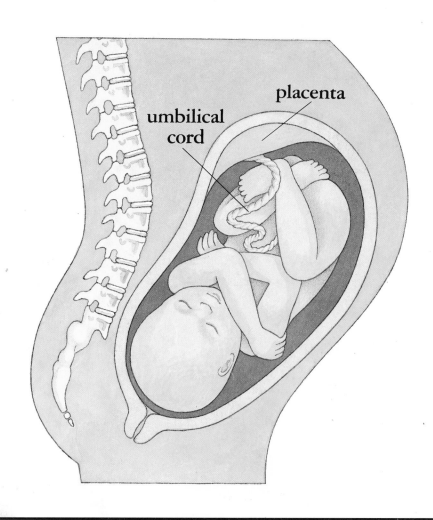

placenta

umbilical cord

Index

About the Author

Gilda Berger is a well-known children's book author of over twenty titles on science subjects, including several that relate to human anatomy and behavior. She grew up in New York City, where she attended City College and earned her B.S. in Special Education. After many years of teaching the learning-disabled and developing reading materials for their use, Ms. Berger decided to devote herself to writing full-time. She and her husband, Mel, who is also an author, reside in Great Neck, New York.

About the Artist

Darcy May is an award-winning illustrator of books for children. A graduate of the Philadelphia College of Art, she has illustrated books for several major publishing houses. Her hobbies include camping, outdoor life, and antiques. She lives in Bucks County, Pennsylvania.